All The Things I Never Said

All The Things I Never Said

Kaylaa' White

To my mom & dad,
thank you for everything, words can't
decribe how much I love y'all.
To Cam & Cortez,
thank you guys for pushing me to be a
good role model.
To my inspirations,
thank you, without you this work
wouldn't exist.

Contents

Dedication	iv
BOYS WILL BE BOYS	1
FAÇADE	2
QUESTIONS	3
DONE.	4
REALITY	5
EXPECTATIONS	6
THE TALE THE HEART TOLD	7
WATER	8
DISTURBANCE IN THE FORCE	9
Persistence	10
GAL+AXY	11
FINALE Of INIQUITY	12
ON GUARD	14
THE ARCHITECT/ GROWTH	16
The Voyage	17
Kingdom	18
MOM	20

Mommy	21
REBELLION	22
Rant(ology); (N) The Study Of Ranting	24
HAIKUS	25
Hypnotic Spring	26
MY OBJECT	27
Rain	28
Ode To Corona.	29
Remember	30
If I Could Tell You.	31
Vale, Sir.	32
Jackie _ _ _ _	33
Pediatric Floor	34
"Draft Saved"	35
AMERIKKKA	36
Who Am I?	37
Am I Next?	38
Author's Note	39

BOYS WILL BE BOYS

A young girl being the subject of ridicule and subjection,
She rolled her eyes,
Let bullies be bullies,
Boys will be boys,
Just ignore them.

She went home crying,
"Why are you always so mean to me?"
"I'm always nice to you."
Only to receive laughter and more jokes in response.
Boys will be boys.

This little girl was taught to keep her weaknesses on the inside,
Don't show your weaknesses on the outside,
Be strong on the outside,
Even though they might hurt you on the inside,
Boys will be boys.

These boys were never told they were wrong,
Growing into men,
Scarring more females, the way they scarred me.

Wounds healing, but the patches of puckered skin,
Left a constant reminder.
Boys will be boys

FAÇADE

I'm a little older now, You accept me with open arms. Your doors of presumed heaven, filled with the deadliest people of all. Most of these girls were probably like me, used to keeping things inside. Unlike me, they used hatred and spite to tear others down, watching them fall in a pile of rubble.

You caused me to doubt myself, I don't look like you, you don't understand me. I belong to a different taxon, but the universal classified me harshly. You didn't like when I had an opinion, you suppressed me, forcing me to compromise and comply.

You accept me with open arms, opening your doors of presumed heaven. While deep in your embrace, I soon realized that I had entered hell.

QUESTIONS

Why can't I be like you?
I straighten my hair, And buy new jeans.

Why can't I be like you?
I stop listening to "ghetto" music, and join team Tay-Tay.

Why can't I be like you?
I like your guys, I pass your tests.

Why can't I be like you?
I became a groupie to your grotesque group.

Why can't I be like you?
Because I am me.

Am I good enough?

DONE.

I am tired of facades,
Emotional barriers I put around
My heart to protect myself
From the reality of my loneliness.

I am tired of pretending
To be happy, smiling,
Saying everything is ok,
When I'm suffering.

I am tired of changing.
Forcing myself to act differently,
Hiding my true feelings to feel
Safe in my chaotic surroundings.

I'm tired of being tired,
When will I be relieved?

REALITY

Loneliness is a state of mind.
It is not a reality.

I have friends,
People care.

Loneliness is a state of mind.
It is not a reality.

Stop isolating yourself,
Make friends.

Loneliness is a state of mind.
It is not a reality.

Why am I so different?
Why can't I fit in?

Loneliness is a state of mind,
but it's my reality.

EXPECTATIONS

I thought I'd fit in with you,
But you didn't accept me either,
Maybe I just don't belong.

A long summer of sadness.
I don't have people to share perspectives,
so, playlist portray pessimistic thoughts,
I'm lonely.

I don't like my body,
Food is bought, I eat enough but,
I'm not happy.

I picked up a pen,
And drafted my thoughts into words,
Every vein my body pulsates with catharsis.
I am one.

THE TALE THE HEART TOLD

The heart told a mysterious tale,
With every pulse,
A new stroke of a pen,

With every beat, a page is turned.

Its stories of happiness and horror
Are told from ear to ear.

Readers are moved by the words
Of assumed fiction.

But the heart knows the truth,
It has felt happiness, horror, pain,
And sorrow.

And throughout it all, it continues to thrive.

WATER

I can't breathe,
someone, please help.
The pressure is too much,
I can't be what you want me to be.
Let me up,
I'm drowning.
Help.
Anyone?
I'm begging please help.
You're not here,
You left me like the rest.
No one cares,
I am alone.
The pressure is too much,
I'm falling.
I can't breathe...

DISTURBANCE IN THE FORCE

When you look at me,
You see a

Smile, a laugh, a grin.

But if you gaze under
The darkened muddy layers
 You will see,

Anger, restlessness, and discontent

These whirlwinds of emotions
Make up the composition that is me.

A silent turbulence,
In a stormy sea.

persistence

I put in long hours,
To get nothing accomplished,
You're my passion, you neglect me.

I'm wasting my life,
Chasing a clouded dream,
That will always be out of my reach.

A cat stuck in a tree,
A kite tangled in a branch.

Should I just give up?

GAL+AXY

I can stay up all night talking to you about,
the sun, the moon, the breeze
gently swaying the trees outside my window
-back and forth.

We're neighboring planets, but galaxies apart.

Retrogrades causing the need
for reconciles and redemption.
You're stubborn, I'm sensitive,
but that doesn't make a difference.

Air and water colliding,
Causing ripples in the oceans of paradise

I can stay up all night talking to you about,
the sun, the moon, the breeze
gently swaying the trees outside my window
-back and forth.

Even though were galaxies apart,
The Uranus, to my Neptune,

We will always exist in my heart.

FINALE of INIQUITY

Our final hours have been
Confusing and Chaotic.
Tangled messes.
Heavy conversations.
Unanswered question.

But in these hours,
I have heeded the words of
Hesitant hushed voices.
Their silent hymns.

We are on hiatus.
We are air and water.
Causing hurling tornados,
Sending emotions soaring into the stars,
Corrupting the orbit of Uranus & Neptune.

We are not meant to be.
Air, you were meant to be free,
Water, I was meant to be grounded,

And although we meet in periods of precipitation,
The rain always stops.
My ¾ are already stretched, and I'm not ready to give up my one.

We're an endless hiatus.
We are not meant to be.

These final hours,
I still care for you in our final hours,
Even in our final hours, I cannot bid you goodbye.

ON GUARD

4/2/18
12:20 am

It feels like I've been waiting on us forever.
But now that I have us,
I don't want you.

You see right through my murky waters,
Making me crystal clear.

You call me on my bluffs,
You see the real me,
The girl I work so hard to protect.

She falls so easily,
She gets so attached,
So, I push you away.

You won't hurt me,
I won't allow you to hurt her.

You see right through my murky waters,
Making me crystal clear.

You call me on my bluffs,
You see the real me,
The girl I work so hard to protect.

You won't hurt her,
I won't allow you to hurt me.

THE ARCHITECT/ GROWTH

I'm building on the construction site of my life.
I put on my hard hat to protect my body,
And I continue on,
The rain prohibits building some days,
But when the ground dries, I continue on.

Just building,
And building,
Until my creation is complete.

The Voyage

The day you left was
cold
and
windy.
I've been preparing for this moment,
you were too good to be true,
and good things don't last for long,

Or at least that's what I've learned
from my experience in friendships
and almost-relationships.

People turn themselves into ships and sail away from me.

Only to let me know of their departure
after they've already reached the horizon.

Kingdom

I was upset that I didn't have...
A small face, and a delicate jawline,
sculpted by the goddess herself.

A petite nose that contoured like
a river, leading to a brow bone that
sits under a dark, slightly arched
thrown, aligned with my outer eye at a diagonal point.

Curves like the Nile,
waves that cascaded down my back,
and light sandy skin to meet at its shore.

But my body is my Kingdom,
I breathe, feel, fear, and love
through this vessel,
my unique gift in this lifetime.

I could change its outer image,
but after that skin sheds,
I'm still left with me.

This body, this soul, this mind.

Accepting myself enabled me
to start living my life.

So excuse me,

If I don't agree with causcasian based beauty standards,
excuse me,
if I won't use parts of my culture to propel myself,
and excuse me,
for not shaming the next female that does.

Her body is her Kingdom, and my body is mine.

MOM

You're my role model,
My protectress,
My friend,
My mom.

I can always count on you
To be there.
My protectress,
My friend,
My mom.

You listen. You understand. You judge.
My friend,
My mom.

I can ask you anything.
My mom

I love you.
My protectress,
My friend,
My mom.

mommy

You feel my voids of sadness,
With rays of vibrant sunshine.

Your precious words of wisdom,
Corrects the errors in my life.

You're beautiful, kind, and understanding,
You're the joy in my life.

The most sacred jewel known to
Mankind,

My favorite person in the entire world

My mom.

REBELLION

I was told racism was over,
That because black people can vote,
And own property,
We should feel equal in today's society.

I was taught America is the land of the free,
Home to 5 percent of the world's population,
But 25% of the world's prisoners.

I was told marijuana was legal,
But POC arrested for possession,
Will have to serve out their sentences.

I was told crime doesn't have a color,
Yet African American males are racially
Profiled every day on the streets.

I was told I should love myself,
But due to appropriation,
People can wear my culture,
And yet I still get called ghetto.

Lies, Lies I know I was told,
But if I speak my mind,
I'm just a rebellious black girl,
In a perfect world.

I am told to love my nation, and I do,

But when I kneel because my nation doesn't love me,
I'm a disgrace.

Lies, Lies I know I was told,
But if I speak my mind,
I'm just a rebellious black girl,
In a perfect world.

I am expected to be thankful for what I have,
to accept my tainted fate with a closed mouth.
Yes, Master.

I am expected to work
seven months into the next year,
To get paid what a male does in the current.
Yes, Master.

I'm expected to learn,
But white students are privileged in education systems,
Leaving the colored to fend for themselves.
Yes Master

Lies, Lies I know I was told,
Twisted realities I was forced to learn.

But if I speak my mind,
I'm just a rebellious black girl,
In a perfect world.

Rant(ology); (n) the study of ranting

Dang, it got to a point we can't wait anymore,
Walmart ain't got the coffee we want,
But they have aisles of watermelon, Sprite,
and chicken that should suffice.

We can't have our children model anymore,
Racial slurs used irrationally,
But I'm supposed to stop thinking negatively,
And accept your apology-

Even though you played with hardships my people had to face.

We can't even say "Black Lives Matter" anymore,
Because we, the inferior, discriminating against the superior.

So, I intentionally, use the word iniquity
Because interestingly,
When we rise, there's always something trying to bring us down.

HAIKUS

Nature
I have allergies.
The pollen makes my nose run.
I do not like spring.

Realization
Racism is trash.
The racists are ignorant.
America please.

Hypnotic Spring

I traveled from my desolate hours of boredom,
And the aurora of spring consumed me,
Dandelions tickling my fingers,
Pulling me deeper into nature's trance.

Tires against tar,
Their rumbling trying to pull me from my bliss,
But the breeze against my arms pushes them away.

I close my eyes,
I hear the crunch of grass under stomping sneakers
Leaves rustling against the branches, as they struggle to break free.

I'm falling further into spring,
The trees,
The flowers,
The breeze beckons me with open arms.

A voice is pulling me from this new-found world.
The scorching sun, and rain clouds let me know
 my time of discovery is coming to an end.

I wave goodbye to my new springtime friends,
And hope for the day we meet again.

MY OBJECT

Before you I was lost.
A cup overflowing with insecurities,
Filled to the brim with self-doubt,
Drowning in the thoughts of others.

I picked up a pen,
My thoughts turned to words
That I could convey to others,
To get them to see me.

Not the *me* I tried to be,
Or the *me* I was forced to be,
But the real, **me.**

The girl who's so awkward she makes people laugh,
The girl who's so liberal she can't conserve water,
The girl who's so undeniably black,
That the mildness of the sun makes her coco buttered melanin glow.
So, I thank you.
Your tangibility, touched my life and made me a better me.
A me I'm still working to be.

Rain

You're a clear sky after
a rainy day-
birds chirping,
my feet sinking into the muddy grass.

She's the smell of dampened earth
that lingers in the air-

a constant reminder that it's spring,
and no matter how sunny it is one day,
the rain is bound to come back,
and wash away the figments of me.

Ode To Corona.

Distance is great when you're
overwhelmed,
upset,
"I need space"

But when the space is too much,
and it feels like these four walls
are moving in closer everyday,
you feel trapped.

Physically
and
Mentally.

Unable to escape from
the constant assault
of your own thoughts.

Remember

Remember when life used to be so simple?

Parent's pre-pricked clothes, and your only concern was saving your best friend a seat on the bus. We smiled wide while missing our two front teeth, unbothered by how we looked, waiting in anticipation for what the tooth-fairy would bring.

When we grew up social media became a thing, and that child-like sense of joy could only be felt on special occasions, now boys reek of hyper-masculinity, and girls: don't be a prude, cover up, but stay sexually appealing.

Everything is just so confusing.

The spaces between us are enormous as society continues to go adrift.

Remember when life used to be so simple?

But you're navigating the difficulties and evolving into the beautiful person you've come to be.

So yeah, reminisce the simplicity , but embrace the difficulty that gives you identity

if I could tell you.

If I could tell you how I feel,
It would be a huge weight off my chest.

The little nothings could possibly become somethings,
and I wouldn't be filled with regret.

"You've got nothing to lose" they say, but
they're wrong,
I could lose you.

Our dynamic could fade and
flame could dwindle leaving no friendship
left to rekindle.

I'm afraid of emabarrasment,
and abandonment,
nothingness.

If I could just tell you how I feel.

Vale, sir.

I'm letting go,
leaving one-sided friendships
in the past, the relationship didn't
last and now I'm only accompanied by your ghost.

I couldn't have you, I convinced
myself that being friends was enough,
but it's hard to go from
having you all of your attention to having none.

When dawn turns to dust,

In the the quiet hours of the night, I think of you,
and all the things we were,
guilt turns into a run on text @2am.

But it's not my fault you chose
who was better for you,
and I won't force a spark that isn't there anymore.

you're a comet that passes the moon.

jackie _ _ _ _

I feel like I never gave you enough credit.
I talk about the ones that made me feel less than my worth,
their actions leaving lasting reminders of how I don't want to be treated.

But you,
you were the perfect gentleman.

I can't bring myself to regret calling things off,
in the end,
I made the best decision for myself,
but that doesn't stop me from thinking about what could've been.

In a perfect world, I could just tell you how I feel
and everything that was paused would resume.
Unfortunately,
I have to face reality,

-I'm leaving
-I can't ever really tell what you're thinking,

and maybe I'm just better off keeping you as a friend.
The friend that could've been- more.

pediatric floor

White ceilings,
the big dewy window,
raindrops slide down it,
like the tears that threaten to escape from my eyes.

It seems like no matter what you're going through,
God never fails to remind you that you're a woman,
here comes the cramps.

I'm thankful,
she's stayed here with me on these uncomfortable beds,
and tried to sleep through the army of nurses
marching into my room.

My thoughts are a battlefield,
i'd be lying if I said I didn't think about what it'd be like if I was dead.

if i just died.

Easier on my family,
easier on me,
I'd be free.

"draft saved"

i don't know what to say to you.
you're going through a tough time,
i want to be there,
but i'm lost,
i don't know where to start.
i remember you said i reminded you of her-
caring about others and neglecting ourselves,
our fear of water,
our love of crime shows,
and my person favorite "old n lit".
you always know what to say when I'm down,
even if i don't explicitly say it.
it's like you just know.

ex: when i was upset about my moon face,
you said you like it and proceeded to compare me to
Alvin & the Chipmunks.
that made me feel better,
and i'm pretty sure you didn't even know what you were doing.

I want you to be great.
I want you to keep growing.
I want you to be everything she would want you to be.
I want you to be happy.

AMERIKKKA

I find it hard to be patriotic right now.
When you have to choose between terrible or worse.
When our country is so divided.

When I can't even look at a person the same after finding out they support Trump.

I know the official term for what I am, (unschooled)
and i don't understand how Christians can support Trump,
to me that seems counterproductive.

I wrote a play where Trump is dead,
but I'm honestly tired of hearing the name Trump.

I hope Biden and Harris can make a difference,
I don't want to say anything is better than Trump,
but the bar is pretty low.
Here's to chucks and pearls.

who am i?

I look at you in reflective surfaces,
I see me,
but who are you?

I see the person you want to be,
and the person you've grown from,
but who are you in this exact moment?

How do you feel?

Are you content?

Are you sad?

Are you broken?

As much as a try, I will never truly know you,

because,

You are ever-changing.
You are me,

And right now,
I don't truly know myself.

am i next?

Will my mother be next?
I close my eyes to keep the tears from falling, but that offers no comfort.

Will my sister be next?

I toss and turn,
only to be met with gruesome scenes from the war against my people, fear, & anguish.

Will my father be next?

I kiss my little brother on the forehead, my love isn't defined by our race, but I know the moment he walks out of the house, that's all they'll see.

Will my brother be next?

We kneeled to peacefully protest, but when they kneel to take a life, they wonder why there's civil unrest.

Will I be next?

You won't listen when we're quiet, and we're tired of years of oppression & being silenced.

So I will keep my fist raised, and shout "I can't breathe" until we break the systematic divide and justice is served, until you SEE ME.

Author's Note

Whoa- you've made is this far. For starters, I just want to thank you so much for reading this. It's always a daunting task to put any of my work out into the world, and I really appreciate you. This past year has been challenging to say the least, and it took a lot of strength and support to stay afloat.

About me...that's hard. Let's put this in list format, because my brain can process that easier.

- I'm from Virginia
- I'm eighteen (Pisces gang)
- I'm a business owner (Young N Lit & Bloom Design Co.)
- I have IBD (Ulcerative Colitis)
- I'll be attending New York University/Tisch in Fall 2021 (Dramatic Writing)

Yeah...I feel like those are the most important things. You can always follow me on Instagram @wildflouwir to see all of my quirkiness up close & personal, and follow my business page @youngnlittt to support the movement. I love you.

Until next time,

-Kaylaa'

www.ingramcontent.com/pod-product-compliance
Lightning Source LLC
Chambersburg PA
CBHW062029290426
44108CB00025B/2832